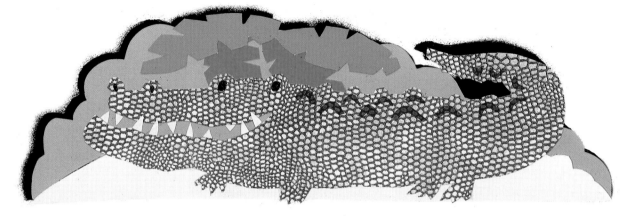

MY ANIMAL FRIENDS

DAVID LE JARS

WORLD BOOK / TWO-CAN

First published in the United States and Canada by
World Book Inc.
525 W. Monroe
20th Floor
Chicago, IL USA
60661
in association with Two-Can Publishing Ltd., 1997

For information on other World Book products, call 1-800-255-1750, x 2238.

ISBN: 0-7166-5903-4 (pbk.)
ISBN: 0-7166-5902-6 (hbk.)
LC: 96-61752

Printed in Spain

1 2 3 4 5 6 7 8 9 10 01 00 99 98 97 96

Art director: Ivan Bulloch
Editor: Diane James
Design Assistant: Dawn Apperley
Illustrator: David Le Jars
Special thanks to Karen Ingebretsen, World Book Publishing

Contents

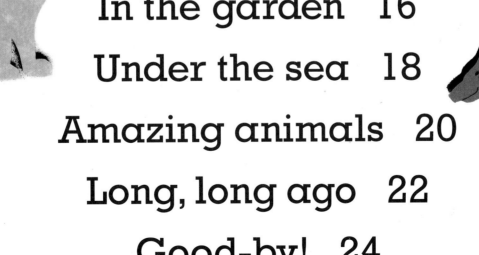

On the farm

goat

horse

How many legs does a horse have?

How many eggs has the chicken laid?

chicken

What noise does a turkey make?

turkey

tractor

sheep

What delicious drink do you get from cows?

pig

cow

Make a hee-haw noise like a donkey.

donkey

Can you find the baby ducks?

duck

ducklings

In the jungle

chimpanzee

sloth

What color are the tiger's stripes?

Which animal do you like best?

tiger

armadillo

crocodile

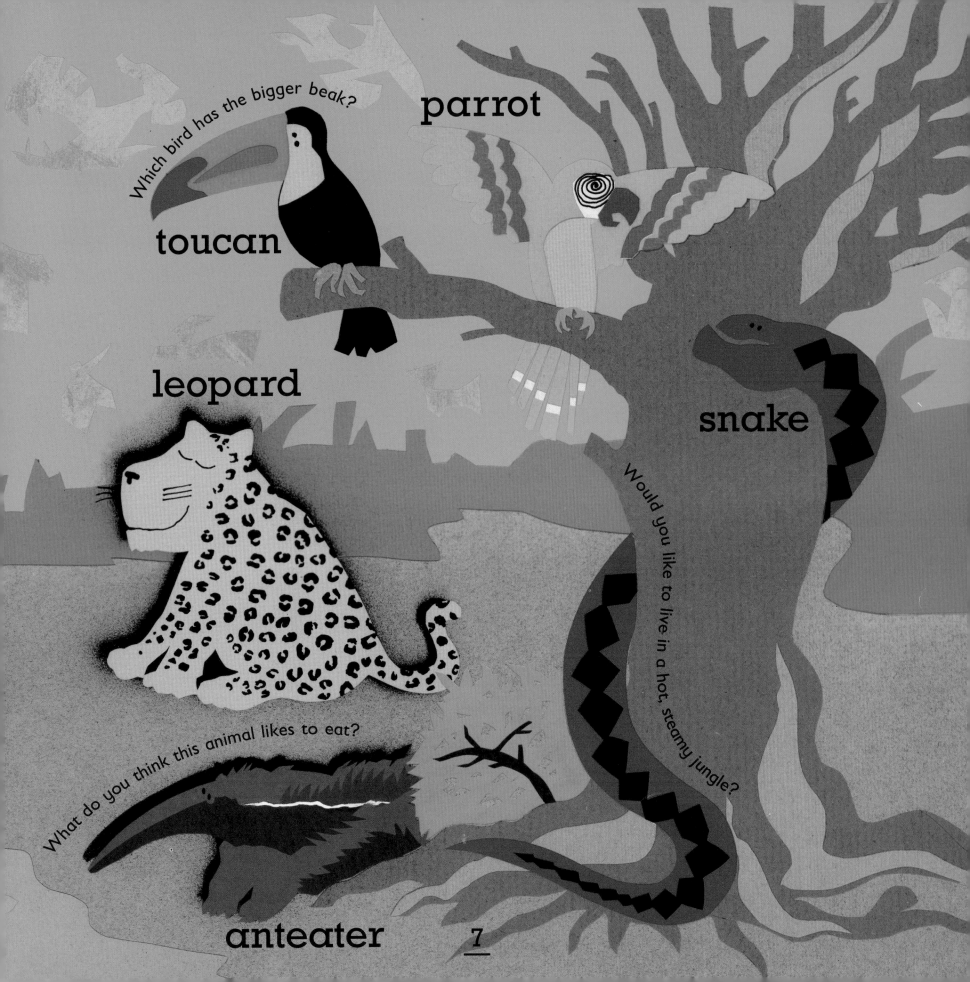

Which bird has the bigger beak?

parrot

toucan

leopard

snake

What do you think this animal likes to eat?

Would you like to live in a hot, steamy jungle?

anteater

Hot and dry

gazelle

Can you run fast like this?

giraffe

rhinoceros

Do you have any clothes with stripes on them?

zebra

baboon

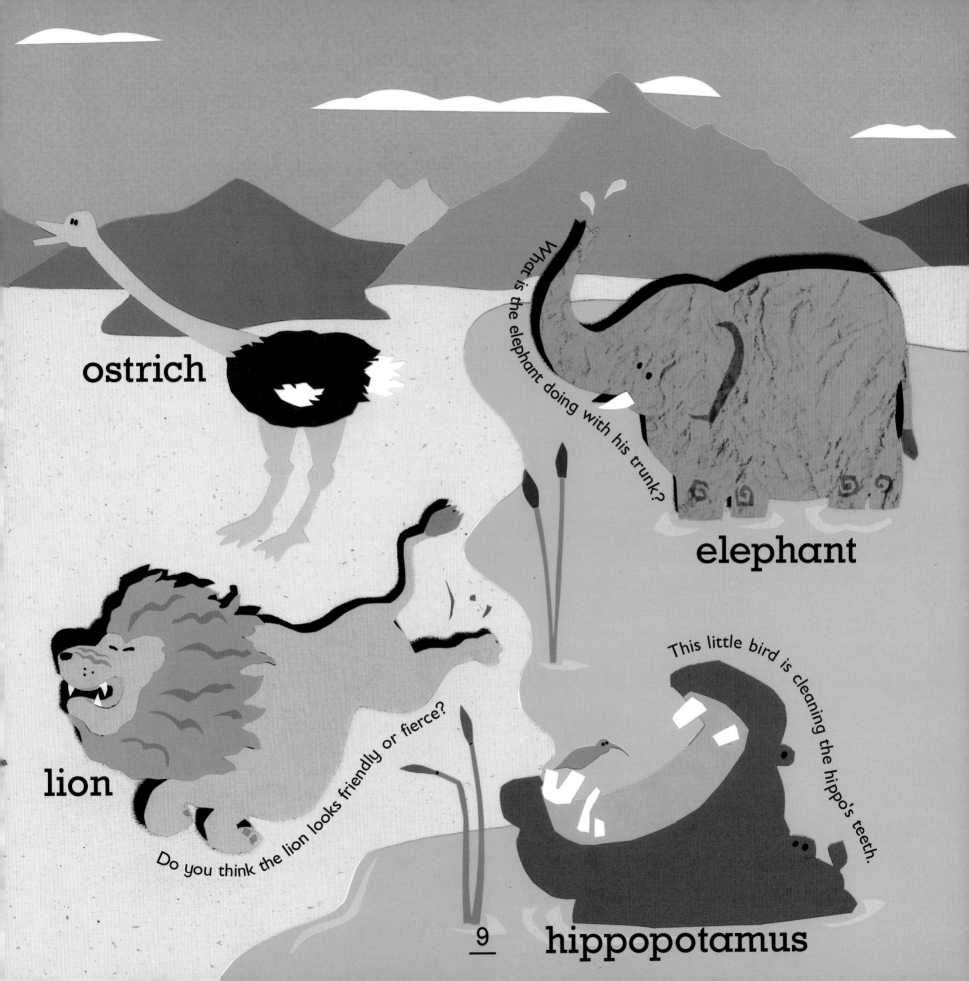

ostrich

What is the elephant doing with his trunk?

elephant

lion

Do you think the lion looks friendly or fierce?

This little bird is cleaning the hippo's teeth.

hippopotamus

Pet store

rat

dog

Can you make a noise like a dog?

canary

rabbit

guinea pig

What do hamsters like to play with?

hamster

What do you call a baby cat?

cat

How many fish are in the tank on the opposite page?

goldfish

Find another bird on this page.

cockatoo

11

Bird watching

What is the eagle having for supper?

eagle

Can you make a noise like an owl?

owl

sea gull

pelican

swan

Wow! What a huge beak.

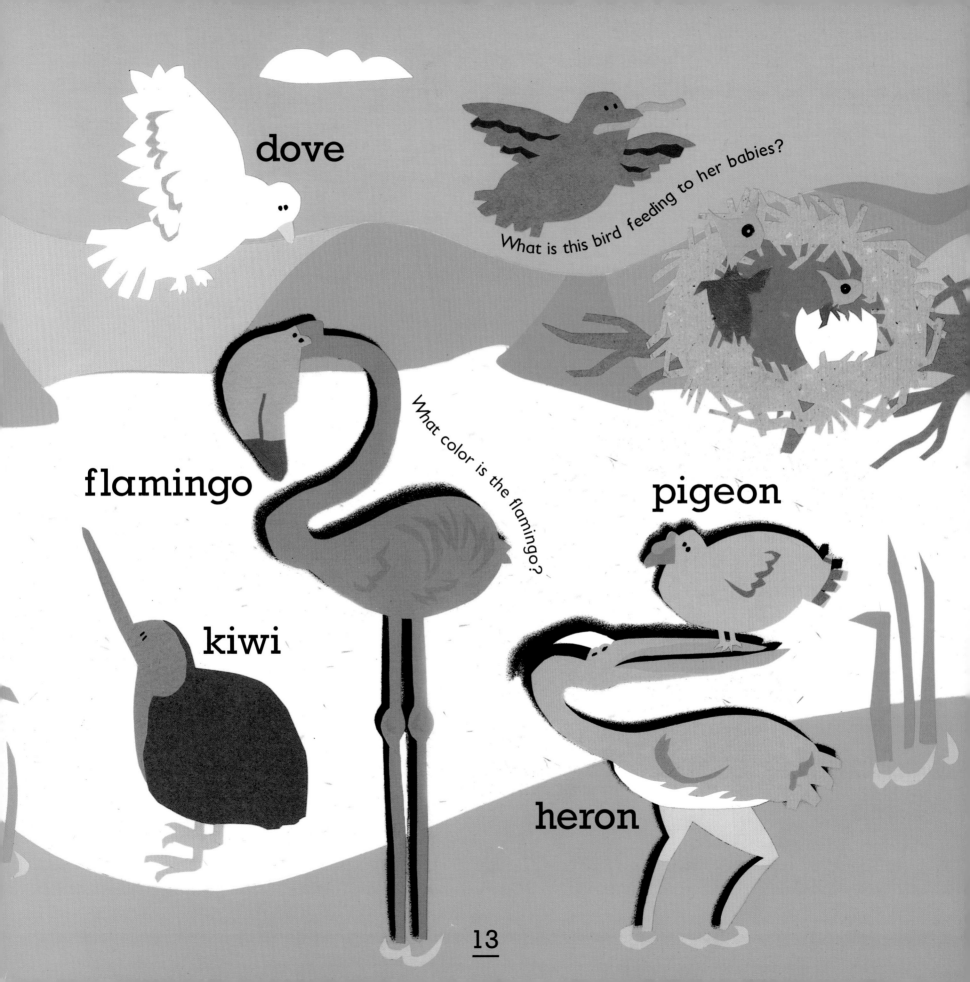

dove

What is this bird feeding to her babies?

flamingo

What color is the flamingo?

pigeon

kiwi

heron

Cold lands

puffin

Find another black-and-white bird.

Inuit

Would you like to live in a house like this?

husky

igloo

reindeer

Look at the reindeer's big antlers!

In the garden

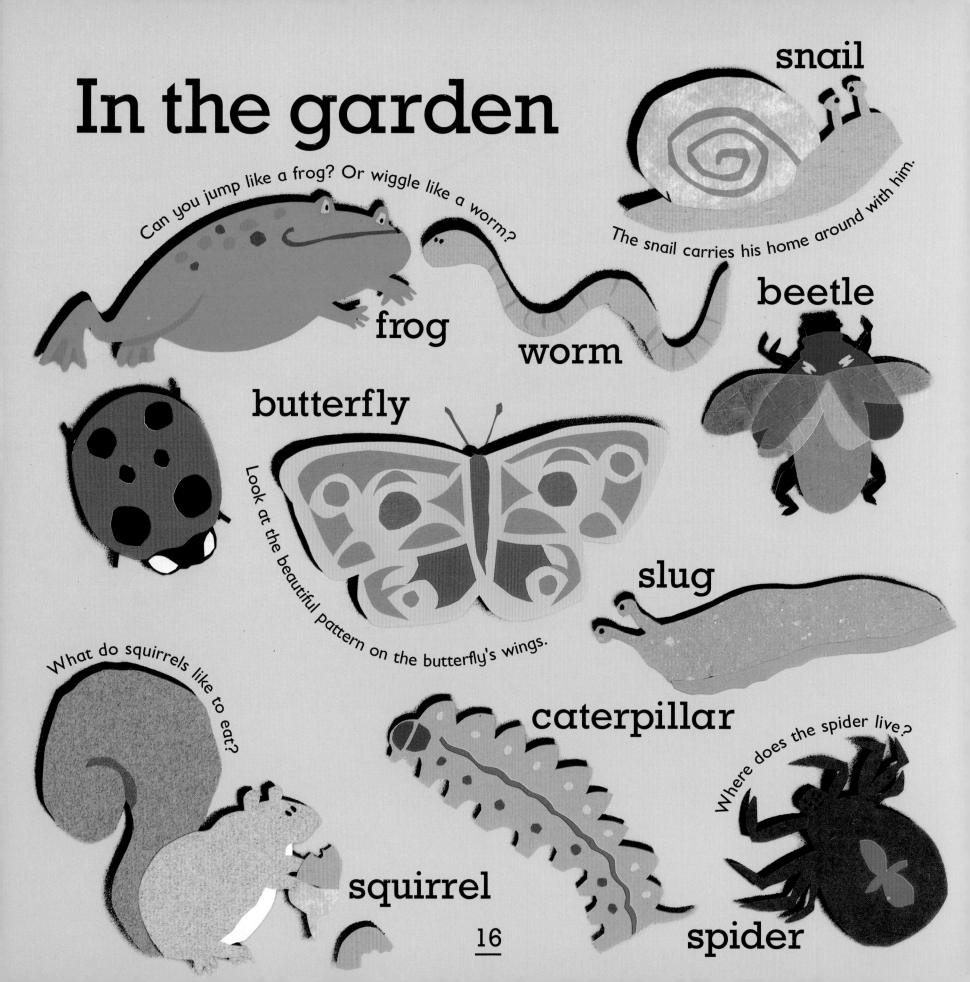

snail

The snail carries his home around with him.

Can you jump like a frog? Or wiggle like a worm?

frog

worm

beetle

butterfly

Look at the beautiful pattern on the butterfly's wings.

slug

What do squirrels like to eat?

caterpillar

Where does the spider live?

squirrel

spider

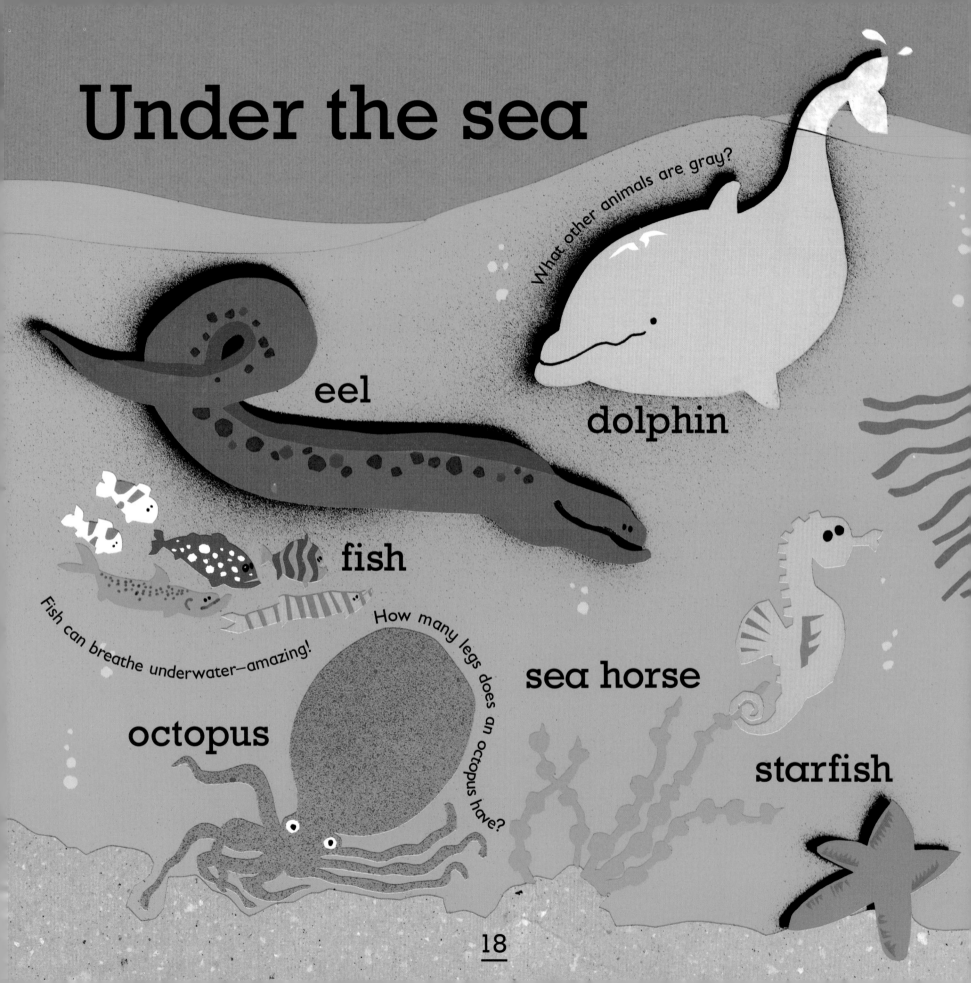

Under the sea

What other animals are gray?

dolphin

eel

Fish can breathe underwater—amazing!

fish

How many legs does an octopus have?

sea horse

octopus

starfish

flying fish

The sea is very, very deep—much deeper than your bath.

jellyfish

zebra fish

shark

Does this look like the gelatin you eat?

Which is your favorite sea creature?

squid

sea anemone

lobster

sea urchin

Shells can be the homes for tiny creatures.

shell

19

Amazing animals

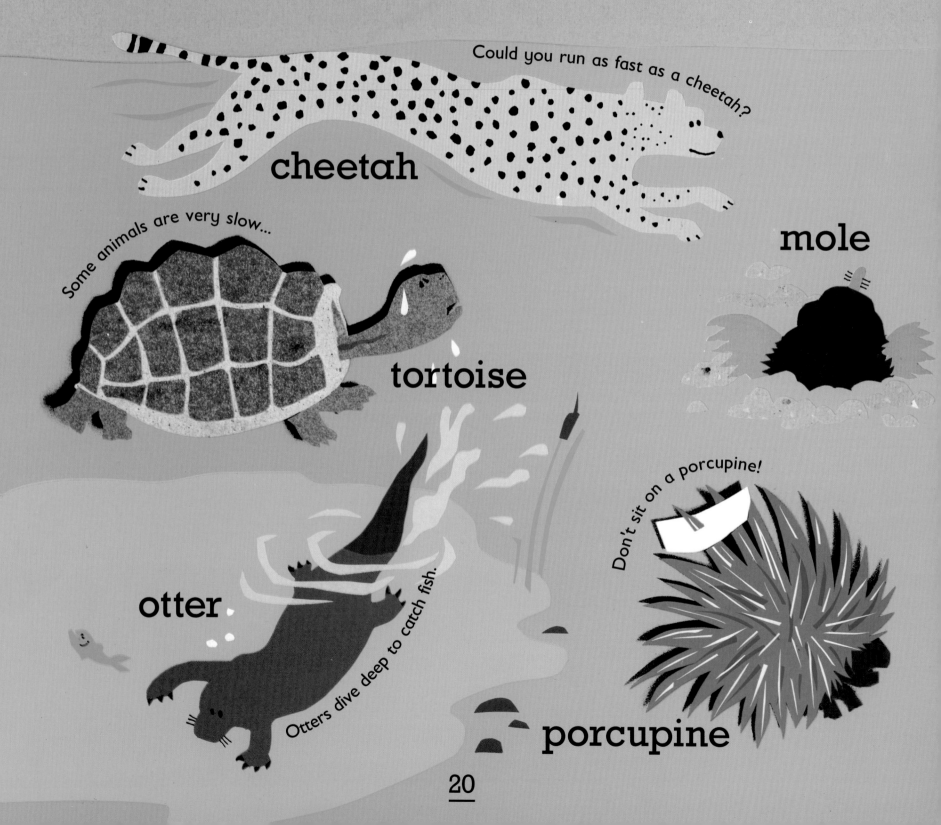

Could you run as fast as a cheetah?

cheetah

mole

Some animals are very slow...

tortoise

otter

Otters dive deep to catch fish.

Don't sit on a porcupine!

porcupine

bat

Why are people afraid of bats?

Where do kangaroo babies live?

koala

kangaroo

Why does the beaver need strong teeth?

beaver

Long, long ago

pterodactyl

plesiosaur

Would you like a dinosaur as a pet?

dimetrodon

Some dinosaurs ate meat and some only ate plants!

stegosaurus

Do you know the name of another animal with a long neck?

brachiosaurus

tyrannosaurus

Are any dinosaurs alive today?

triceratops

Good-by!

zzzz... hee-haw... croak... oink...
mooooo... squawk... meow...
woof woof... cluck... sssss...